Where Do Creatures Sleep at Night?

To Ford, Georgina, Teddy, and Jack, with so much love!—S. J. S.

To all the soft and (sometimes) warm things that get sleepy—
with fur, feathers, wings, scales, long tongues, manes, or hair—
including all my grandchildren.—R. E. H.

Where Do Creatures Sleep at Night?

Steven J. Simmons

Illustrated by **Ruth E. Harper**

iɴi Charlesbridge

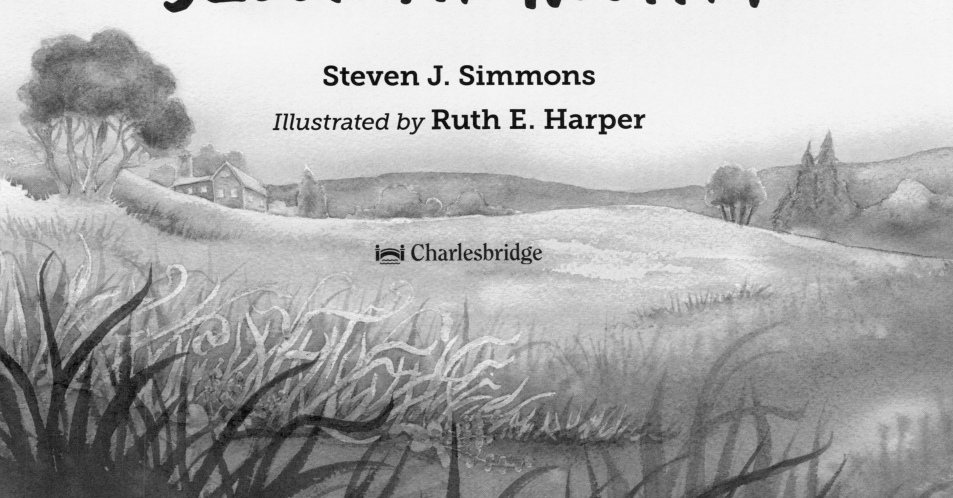

We are used to seeing creatures by day.
But where at night do you think they stay?
Do they sit or stand or roll up real tight?
Or wake in the dark with a terrible fright?

Do they hide in a bush or perch in a tree?
Do they huddle with friends where we cannot see?
Let's take a look at what creatures do
when you are asleep and the day is through. . . .

A butterfly's wings flutter all day,
yet at night they are softly folded away.
The butterfly finds a branch or a bush
where it can stay while all goes *shushhh*.

With tiny clawed feet, it hangs upside down,
making it difficult to be found.

Honeybees are buzzing much of the day,
gathering nectar, then flying away.
Making honey back in the hive,
they need this sweet food to survive.

They stop their work to get some sleep,
head down for hours without a peep.
Their antennae droop to the floor . . .
until they awake and go out once more.

A frog can jump high or croak out loud
or balance on a lily pad under a cloud.
It has a slippery, icky wet back
and a sticky tongue to catch bugs for a snack.

No one knows if it really does sleep,
but a frog rests for hours, not moving its feet.

A goldfish swims in its bowl all day,
gulping the food that drops its way.
But in the darkness, deep in the night,
it may drift to the bottom till morning's light.

It stays very still to get a good rest
so when it arises it will be at its best.

Its eyes stay open, and here's why that's true:
goldfish have no eyelids. What else can they do?

Ducks paddle around with webbed feet.

Hear them quack, quack, quack as you throw them a treat.

At night, sometimes, they sleep in a line.
And at each end, a duck opens one eye
to make sure the others are safe
and to sound the alarm before it's too late!

Birds soar as far as the eye can see.

Imagine the view from the top of a tree!

If it gets cold, they do something neat:

they puff up their feathers to keep in the heat.

When birds have babies, they build a nest
to protect their young and get some rest.
Other times they'll settle on a bush, branch, or vine,
or under a bridge, where they will sleep fine.

Horses gallop with wind in their mane.

They'll eat from your hand—carrots or grain.

But unlike most animals, they can sleep on their feet,

and they won't fall over while they are asleep.

They can do this at night or during the day,
in a stable or field or wherever they stay.

A tree squirrel darts and flicks its tail,
looking for nuts on a grassy trail.
It may lie in the sun on a warm day.
If you get too close, it will scurry away.

At night it is tired and finally free
to sleep in a den inside of a tree
or on a branch where it's built a drey.
Both seem like cozy places to stay.

Have you seen rabbits hop up and down
and use their front paws to dig holes in the ground?
Rabbits play with friends in a field
and nibble on grass if they need a meal.

When it's time for rabbits to rest,
they can hop into their holes, where they sleep best.

Cats can jump or pounce on toys,
chase a mouse, and purr with joy,
drink some water from a bowl,
stretch their legs, or take a stroll.

Cats sleep most of the time,
day or night—either is fine.
Whether nook or chair or cozy bed,
they will find a place to rest their head.

Dogs are such fun, as you might know.
They run and they play and love you so.

Their nose can sniff out things underground
better than we can, as you may have found.
Dogs aren't picky: they can sleep on the floor.
But if you let them in bed, watch out—they might snore!

Children like you do lots of things,
from playing ball to going on swings,
reading a book or building with blocks,
riding a bike or sliding in socks.

Then at night, after you're fed,
you snuggle up in your own sweet bed!

GOOD NiGHT!

SLEEP TIGHT!

A note from the author: Sleep is important for all children. By sleeping, you rest your body and mind, which helps you grow. And just as the creatures in this book sleep in order to be full of energy the next day, so must you!

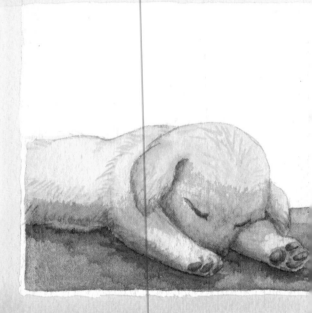

Text copyright © 2021 by Steven J. Simmons
Illustrations copyright © 2021 by Ruth E. Harper
All rights reserved, including the right of reproduction in whole or in part in any form.
Charlesbridge and colophon are registered trademarks of Charlesbridge Publishing, Inc.

At the time of publication, all URLs printed in this book were accurate and active. Charlesbridge, the author, and the illustrator are not responsible for the content or accessibility of any website.

Published by Charlesbridge
9 Galen Street, Watertown, MA 02472
(617) 926-0329 • www.charlesbridge.com

Printed in China
(hc) 10 9 8 7 6 5 4 3 2 1

Illustrations done in Daniel Smith watercolors on Arches paper
Display type set in Underland Sans by Wacaksara Co.
Text type set in Museo Slab by Jos Buivenga
Color separations by Colourscan Print Co Pte Ltd, Singapore
Printed by 1010 Printing International Limited in Huizhou, Guangdong, China
Production supervision by Jennifer Most Delaney
Designed by Diane M. Earley

Library of Congress Cataloging-in-Publication Data
Names: Simmons, Steven J., 1946– author. | Harper, Ruth E., illustrator.
Title: Where do creatures sleep at night? / Steven J. Simmons; illustrated by Ruth Harper.
Description: Watertown, MA: Charlesbridge, 2021. | Audience: Ages 3-7 | Audience: Grades K-1 | Summary: "Learn where creatures such as a frog, duck, horse, and squirrel sleep at night in informational verse."—Provided by publisher.
Identifiers: LCCN 2020051093 (print) | LCCN 2020051094 (ebook) | ISBN 9781580895217 (hardcover) | ISBN 9781632898456 (ebook)
Subjects: LCSH: Sleep behavior in animals—Juvenile literature. | Animals—Habitations—Juvenile literature. | Animal behavior—Juvenile literature. | Sleep—Juvenile literature.
Classification: LCC QL755.3 .S56 2021 (print) | LCC QL755.3 (ebook) | DDC 591.5/19—dc23
LC record available at https://lccn.loc.gov/2020051093
LC ebook record available at https://lccn.loc.gov/2020051094